THE
MISCONCEPTIONS
of
HUMILITY

THE MISCONCEPTIONS of HUMILITY

Kartriece Ward

The Misconceptions of Humility
Copyright © 2025 Kartriece Ward
All rights reserved.

No part of this book may be reproduced, stored in a retrieval system, or transmitted in any form or by any means—electronic, mechanical, photocopying, recording, or otherwise—without prior written permission from the publisher, except in the case of brief quotations embodied in critical articles or reviews.

ISBN: 978-1-7353198-2-7
Library of Congress Control Number: 2025901902
Printed in the United States of America

For permissions, inquiries, or more information, contact:
hello@kartrieceward.com
www.MisconceptionsOfHumility.com

In His Hands Publications.

Unless otherwise indicated, all Scriptures are taken from the King James Version (KJV): Public domain. New King James Version (NKJV): Scripture taken from the New King James Version®. Copyright © 1982 by Thomas Nelson. Used by permission. All rights reserved. New International Version (NIV): Scripture taken from the Holy Bible, New International Version®, NIV®. Copyright © 1973, 1978, 1984, 2011 by Biblica, Inc.™ Used by permission. All rights reserved worldwide. GOD'S WORD® (GW): Scripture taken from GOD'S WORD®, © 1995 God's Word to the Nations. Used by permission of God's Word Mission Society. All rights reserved.

Cover Design and Interior Design
by Visions Promotional Agency
www.vpromoagency.com

To my spiritual leaders, both past and present.

…warn an understanding person, and he will gain more knowledge.

Proverbs 19:25b GW

Contents

INTRODUCTION 9

HUMILITY 11

TRUSTING GOD WITH ALL 14

WAITING ON GOD? 19

LEVELS OF VULNERABILITY 21

LET YOUR LIGHT SHINE, BUT NOT TOO BRIGHT 29

DON'T THINK OF YOURSELF HIGHLY 32

BLESSED TO BLESS, NOT RECEIVE? 33

THE INITIATOR 35

PRAYER OF REPENTANCE 46

GUIDE ME BY MO JCKSN 47

ABOUT THE AUTHOR... 50

INTRODUCTION

This is not your typical book about pride or humility. This is a step beyond the common items mentioned around humility. As we dissect each of the misconceptions, receive with an open heart and mind. Prayerfully, this book will challenge you to do a deep self-examination within, like a mirror check with the Word of God around the misconceptions of humility. If you read this book with the mindset that you already know everything rather than viewing it as a helpful reminder, you should check your heart posture. The subtle aspects are what we are dealing with in this book… not the obvious.

A couple of years ago, the Lord gave me this book project, and by His grace, it is now published! It includes a part of my testimony—shared solely for the glory of God—and features a song that means so much to me, entitled *"Guide Me"* by Mo JCKSN. (Be sure to check the section in the back for instructions on how to redeem your very own copy of *Guide*

Me, included with your purchase of this book.) I'm convinced both the song and book will be a blessing to many by the grace of God because it is God's idea for sure. May God bless you as we embark on this journey together.

*They won the victory over him because of
the blood of the lamb and the word of their testimony.
They didn't love their life so much that
they refused to give it up.*

Revelation 12:11 GW

HUMILITY

Humility is often thought of as taking the low road or not thinking of yourself more highly than you should. Although both are a part of humility, there is much more than what meets the eye. Pride, which is the opposite of humility, has a sneaky way of sliding in and rearing its ugly little head, and unfortunately, even under the mindset of one thinking, they are indeed being humble.

This very misconception can keep you from going to the next level with God. He despises pride. Pride can take many different forms, including being wrapped in what could be perceived as a garment of humility.

We are going to deal with the misconceptions of humility. You know, the parts of humility you may not have thought of as anything more than being humble. Misconception is a view or opinion that is incorrect because it's based on faulty thinking or understanding. Therefore, we are dealing with the parts that remain *after* you've intentionally and subconsciously made sure you're being humble but didn't realize the undetected layers disguised as humility.

WHAT IS IT REALLY?

To be clear on what humility is, according to the Oxford English Dictionary, humility is defined as 'a modest or low view of one's own importance; humbleness.' Merriam-Webster defines humble as 'not proud or haughty: not arrogant or assertive.' This is the way I typically thought of humility.

Culturally, in the westernized southern black churches and from some "church people," we were taught to be humble and that you must humble yourself, which is accurate. The Bible does state in 1 Peter 5:6 KJV, "Humble yourselves therefore, under the mighty hand of God..." We're also instructed in James 4:10 ESV to humble yourselves before the Lord, and he will exalt you. The impression given by some in the church was that being humble meant things like you were not supposed to be able to look stylish and exude confidence even through your appearance. It would be considered doing too much. Another example is the instruction to humbly wait on God, but sometimes excluding the fact that, in a lot of cases, God is waiting on you. Even if this was more of a subconscious message being sent, it could be perceived across the board.

The issue is when we do not allow Holy Spirit to guide us when navigating that thin line between arrogance and confidence, the thin line between being humble and the false sense of humility, the thin line between trusting God and partially trusting God. Humility is not just for those who may be serving in some capacity. It is for everyone; no one is exempt from the requirement of humbling themselves.

heart checks

- Do you recognize anything in your life that resembles misconceived humility? If so, what part?
- In what area can you allow Holy Spirit to guide you?

TRUSTING GOD WITH ALL

Trust is a major factor in walking in biblical humility. We have to trust in God and who he is. Trusting Him due to knowing who he is, we can better trust him with our lives and in every area of our lives. The misconception comes in when we think we aren't operating in pride when we say, "Here, God, I trust you with all, with everything but 'that.'" "That" could mean a ton of different things because it varies based on the individual.

Ask yourself, "Are my actions showing I trust God with all OR all but 'that'?" Be honest with yourself and even ask God to reveal to you any areas you are withholding "that" from him. It literally could be anything, such as finances, relationships, your health, etc. For me, it was my emotions. Little did I know I was operating in pride by subconsciously trying to control part of my life. I didn't know this until God led me to a mountain top experience up north in the USA and then led me to the Mideast USA shortly after.

It is prideful to think we do not need God in a certain area of our life. We need God in every area. We need Holy Spirit to brood over us and guide us into all truth. Without God, we are nothing, and so we make our boast in the Lord and not in ourselves or other people.

SIDE NOTE ON TRUSTING GOD WITH MY FINANCES

The thing is, we must rest in knowing that God is Alpha and Omega, the beginning and the end. He is all-knowing, all-seeing, omnipotent, omnipresent, and we should want to trust him with our all. Not just parts of it. One of the struggles I discovered I needed to overcome was not fully trusting God with my finances. I knew he was my source, but when times were tough financially, it was easy to get off track subconsciously thinking it was better for me to attempt to use the 10% which was his to help pay the present bill versus trusting he was able to help me do more with my 90% than for me to do something with my 100% without his blessing. This is a form of pride to dare think that anything outside of the plan or will of God was the best plan. God wants us to surrender ALL things, including the finances, which is simply a form of exchange on earth. As for our Heavenly Father, He, too, has a currency He provides in His kingdom for exchanging, and that currency is faith. We must have faith and believe God has our best interest at heart.

heart checks

- Are your actions showing you trust God with all OR all but 'that'?
- What are some ways you can know if you desire to move forward with trusting God?
- Are you allowing God to be your source and not just your resource?

TRUSTING GOD WITH MY HEART

Of course, Proverbs tells us to trust the Lord with all of our heart and lean not unto our own understanding but in all our ways acknowledge him, and he will direct our path.

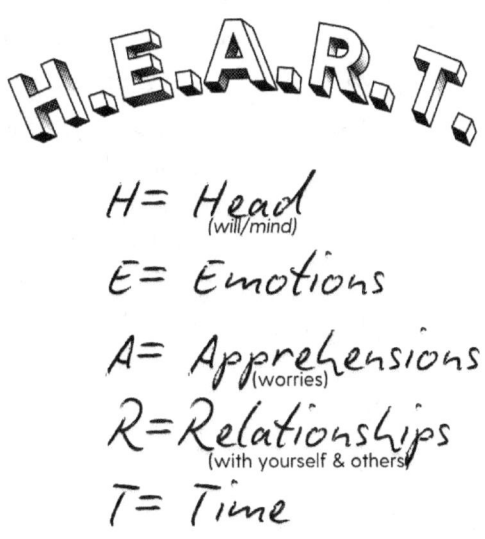

The Lord gave me an acronym for the word "heart" regarding what he was requiring of me when he said to trust him with my heart. ALL of my heart. He wanted my **H**ead, which was considered my will and mind. God wanted my **E**motions. He wanted my **A**pprehensions as well, which were my worries. God wanted me to trust him with my

Relationships, not only with myself but with others. For the "T," God wanted my **Time.** In some ways, it might seem easier, but unless you let go of trying to handle it on your own and fully cast your cares on God—who cares deeply for you—it won't truly be as easy. The level of pride that is present for us to have the audacity to think we can keep doing life without him in every area is wild. Especially when He has a plan in place to order our steps and direct our paths, combatting the way we may regularly see fit to do things.

Casting all our cares on the Lord is an act of trust, for He truly cares for us. God can be trusted with our whole hearts, and He lovingly invites us to lay all our burdens at His feet.

heart checks

- Are my actions reflecting I'm trusting God with all of my heart?
- Pause for a moment and write anything that may come to mind that you may need to relinquish to the Lord around the five areas.

WAITING ON GOD?

Have you ever told someone, "Chile, I'm waiting on the Lord..."? But were you really? Sometimes, the Lord is waiting on us, yet we use the term as a crutch or an excuse for procrastination. For clarity, in this context, we are not speaking of the type of wait the scripture refers to when it says, "Those that wait on the Lord shall renew their strength..." We are discussing the type of self-imposed waiting that can prolong the process. Granted, everything is spiritual, and if you were unaware, consider this your heads up or your notification: **E-V-E-R-Y-T-H-I-N-G** is spiritual. So yes, sometimes you may be coming against the spirit of delay, the spirit of fear, etc., but at times, it's simply because we don't know who we are or whose we are. We must be able to discern when it's God or when it is us. The misconception is that waiting on God as described above isn't actually a form of procrastination. To procrastinate regarding the assignments from God is a form of pride, as it reflects the audacity one has to believe they have all the time in the world to keep putting it off. When in actuality, the word of God lets us know in Ecclesiastes 9:10 KJV, "Whatsoever thy hand findeth to do, do it with thy might; for there is no work, nor device, nor knowledge, nor wisdom, in the grave whither thou goest." In other words, we don't know when it will be our time to go, and we want to have completed everything the Lord gave us to do and fulfill our assignment on this earth. So, to put it off like we have all the time does not make sense.

Let us choose to not only rest in the finished work of Jesus Christ regarding some of the things we are waiting on God to do; Let us also choose not to procrastinate regarding the thing God has called us to do in this hour. We don't want to unknowingly be prideful and keep ourselves away from the protection and covering that comes with walking in obedience.

heart checks

- Are you waiting for God to do something he has already done?
- What are some of the things God has instructed you to do that you haven't done yet?
- Are you going to walk in complete obedience or partial obedience, which is still a form of disobedience?

LEVELS OF VULNERABILITY

God is so gracious that through Holy Spirit, he is constantly working on us and our character when we allow him to. In a dream one of the things God prompted me to work on was my level of vulnerability in preparation for my husband's arrival. One thing is for sure: my husband is going to be grateful for Holy Spirit and for my workout trainer! Both have been doing a number on me, and I'm not only better for it but extremely grateful. What does this have to do with the misconceptions of humility, you may ask? There is a certain level of vulnerability you need to have with the Lord. Holy Spirit literally had to train me, and I am constantly learning. Thankfully, there are ways for us to be able to be vulnerable with God and with ourselves that will, in turn, allow us to be vulnerable with other people in a healthy way.

I am a pretty private person for the most part, but when God tells you to share, you share. You never know the impact your story can have on someone else that needs to hear it. For me, this level of sharing is a bit foreign. As an adolescent, I was taught to have thick skin, which is a bit of a blessing but a not so positive trait when it's not balanced with emotional support. With time, I subconsciously suppressed my emotions and eventually, without realizing it, didn't share much in great detail with others when it came to emotional vulnerability. This resulted in years of not being able to cry. My tear ducts still worked because my eyes would water when cutting onions and if something flew into my eyes, but other than that, I couldn't cry. I was much like the character in the movie *The Holiday*, featuring Cameron Diaz and Jack Black. Cameron's character couldn't cry anymore since she was a child. Like her, even when I tried to cry, I couldn't, and when crying would try to come up, it couldn't get past some sort of subconscious internal barrier.

VULNERABLE WITH GOD

About a month and a half before an event called Kingdom Camp occurred, I heard about it and sensed God was leading me to go. Everything lined up for me to go, and off I went by myself to the mountains to seek God with an organization that I had been introduced to via a Christian business conference only a couple of months prior. Not knowing the exact reason for my being there, I was in full expectation of the possibility of what God had in store for me. He did not disappoint. Everything was amazing, the people were kind, and I knew I was supposed to be there that weekend. It was during that weekend that God began to reveal my "that" to me. While pressing in, there seemed to be something keeping me from tapping all the way in.

One of the nights, I literally went to the car and expressed to God my desperate need to know what the problem was and what was hindering me. I was receiving while there, but there was something holding me back that I couldn't pinpoint. At my "enough is enough" moment—when I had done all I knew to do—I asked God if I was broken, wondering if that was the problem. It was as though His response was, "No, that IS the problem."

VULNERABLE WITH GOD & MYSELF

It was as if God was letting me know, *No, that was the problem—I wasn't broken.* I was always trying to keep it all together, even before Him, in His presence. That realization got me thinking and self-examining during the rest of my time at Kingdom Camp. I repented and prayed for clarity and for Him to reveal what needed to change. During the last session, Apostle mentioned as a sidenote during his message, "*Fire Extinguishers,*" about how pride is a sneaky thing that can creep up subtly. Immediately, it was highlighted to me as though my search antennas went off. I made a note to study that out more and find out what God wanted me to know.

OBEDIENCE BRINGS PROVISION

While on the mountain top up north during Kingdom Camp, literally while praying to the Lord corporately, back home, the Lord spoke to someone at that moment to sow a 4 figure financial seed into my life. Of course, I was unaware until the next day, but when I found out, I was in amazement of God. To know that while on the mountaintop seeking His face, God was orchestrating things on my behalf, I was so grateful. When I was asking God what he wanted me to do with the money, after a while, it was like he was saying, "You said you needed the resources to go, didn't you? Here you go." That was in reference to desiring to go Midwest for New Year's Eve weekend to connect with the same people who hosted the camp. At first, it seemed like a long shot because the flights were so expensive. Eventually, I found some decent flight and hotel prices within my budget, and I was able to not only book but extend my stay for a sabbatical to pray and fast.

VULNERABLE WITH GOD, MYSELF AND OTHERS

While there, we literally prayed the new year in. Again, I felt like I was at the right place at the right time. That's where I was supposed to be. We prayed to leave certain things in that year and refused to bring them into the new year. The next day Apostle preached a powerful message about the theme for the upcoming year. When I returned to my car, my heart was so full, full of gratitude for what I just received. Later that evening, as I was recording a recap video and reflecting, I was feeling overwhelmed with gratitude. I stopped the recording to investigate what was happening. My eyes started getting watery as I was reflecting on God. Then, to the point I could not hold it back, this slightly salty liquid substance began to stream down my face. It wasn't a big, ugly cry, and although it didn't last long at all, I asked Holy Spirit to help me navigate the moment because I didn't know how to manage it or what to do. He had me play some worship music, and I continued to thank God for who He is and for never giving up on me. It was a huge breakthrough because I hadn't cried in years, and I mean years. Although this liquid substance streamed down my face briefly, it was the fact that I could not suppress the feeling. I couldn't stop the tears. I am forever grateful. I indeed received my deliverance and am forever changed. So, if you see me shedding a few tears here and there, thank God with me and just know it is a sign of what the Lord has done for me.

I believe this was a compilation of His Word to me via the dream earlier in the year and obedience. By the grace of God, from that point, I was directed to attend the conference.

From there, I was introduced to the ministry of the leaders who host Kingdom Camp, went to the mountaintop up north to seek God more, and had the seed planted to study the subtle ways of pride—studying it, doing pride devotionals, etc. and I then went to the Midwest, praying against certain things and leaving it in the past. Then the next day, I heard the sermon that left me with such a high level of gratitude and freedom, I couldn't hold back the tears. Indeed, ALL GLORY TO GOD.

A scripture in Joel literally summarized what happened, and I wasn't even looking for the scripture, and honestly, I'm not sure if I'd ever read it prior to that day. While I was still in the Midwest, it was like Holy Spirit was confirming my experiences for me in the word of God. All honor to God.

Joel 2:12-13 KJV says,

> "[12] Therefore also now, saith the LORD, turn ye even to me with all your heart, and with fasting, and with weeping, and with mourning:
>
> [13] And rend your heart, and not your garments, and turn unto the LORD your God: for he is gracious and merciful, slow to anger, and of great kindness, and repenteth him of the evil."

There are seven things I want you to notice in Joel 2:12-13.

1. The time is now. God is letting us know not to put off to tomorrow what we can do today. In this case, now is the time to examine our hearts for any subtle or inconspicuous pride.

2. Turn and come to God with **ALL** of your heart. Draw close to Him with every part of you—including your head (your will and mind), your emotions and apprehensions (worries), your relationships, and your time. Bring even the things you may be ashamed of, as well as the parts of yourself that feel too late to change. **Everything**.

3. Return to God with fasting.

4. And return weeping.

5. Let your broken heart show your sorrow.

6. Return in repentance to the Lord your God.

7. God is merciful, patient, keeps his promises, slow to anger, and always ready to forgive vs only straight punishment.

heart checks

- What is your level of vulnerability with the Lord? With yourself? With others?
- Are there any areas in your life that currently require you to do as it says in Joel 2:12-13?

LET YOUR LIGHT SHINE, BUT NOT TOO BRIGHT

Of course, as Christians, those who are Christ-like, we are to let our light shine. We are indeed the light of the world according to Matthew 5:14, just like a city that sits on a hill cannot be hid. The misconception is often one may have to dim their light so it doesn't offend someone else. Let your light shine. We are not supposed to conceal our light but let it shine.

The misconception is we are not supposed to let our light shine brightly in certain arenas, such as our workplace or the things we do in business as if it was a form of humility. It is not. Jesus lets us know if we are ashamed of him, he will be ashamed of us before His Father in Heaven. Don't try to hide what the Lord is doing in and through your life. Let it shine to represent him.

The other part of letting our light so shine before men is for them to see our good works according to Matthew 5:16

and glorify our Father above. Works in this passage mean business, employment, any product accomplished by hand, art industry or mind, and an act or deed. I used to feel like it would be a form of "putting my chest out" or drawing too much attention to myself to promote some of my work or products.

One of my business mentors put it like this: they said something to the extent of, "If you have a product you know is a solution for someone's problem and you don't let them know about it, you are doing them an injustice." Especially when you know they need it and are in search of a solution. If "works" means your business and/or products, then as you let your light shine, people will be drawn to it to see it and glorify our Father above. Show to shine to glorify God.

Sometimes, when a person is shining their light, others may not always see it as a good thing. We are not supposed to dim our lights just so others feel more comfortable around us. It may even be seen as a form of boasting, but when shining our light correctly, it's not a boast in ourselves or our abilities but a boast in the Lord. We are supposed to make our boast in the Lord, and the humble hear thereof and be glad, according to Psalm 34:2.

We don't want to be a hindrance to others or a hindrance to God receiving his glory. Allow God to use you as he desires.

heart checks

- Have you been dimming your light?
- In what way(s) can you let your light shine bright?
- Is there an assignment the Lord gave you to develop and execute that you have been delaying?

DON'T THINK OF YOURSELF HIGHLY

According to Romans 12:3a NIV, "For by the grace given to me I say to every one of you: Do not think of yourself more highly than you ought," The bible does not mention you should not think of yourself highly, it says more highly than you should. The misconception is we should shy away from speaking highly of ourselves, but instead, we should have a level of confidence. A confidence of not only who we are but whose we are. When we adopt that mentality, it helps us to stand firm no matter where we are or what we are faced with. Our confidence comes from our creator. We are made in the image of God. That alone sets a different benchmark than what our natural minds may perceive. The perception of ourselves will always be challenged, which is why it is crucial to find our identity in the Word of God.

BLESSED TO BLESS, NOT RECEIVE?

We are blessed to be a blessing to other people. That is for sure. We are meant to be able to share with others what we have. On the same token, we must be able to receive. The Lord tells us in Luke 6:38a, "Give and it shall be given unto you; good measure, pressed down, and shaken together, and running over, shall men give into your bosom..." The misconception comes when one has a hard time receiving. Some people give, give, and give but have a hard time receiving. Does that mean we are blessed to bless but not to receive, too? No way. The difficulty in receiving could be more than humility. Pride can often prevent us from receiving help or even asking for it. When we allow the pressures of past experiences to lead us to believe that we can only depend on ourselves, we miss the opportunity to rely on God and receive His blessings in whatever form He chooses. Sometimes, a person can feel unworthy, causing them to feel as though they don't deserve what is being offered or given to them. This goes back to trusting God to meet whatever need you have, however, he wants to, and also knowing who God has called you to be. Remember, God can be trusted, and by the grace of God, you are enough, and you deserve to receive as well.

Sometimes, people have a hard time being able to receive, and at times, it is wrapped in pride when they feel bad for receiving. We have to check our heart motives to get to the reason as to why we may not like to receive. Are you being prideful and not wanting someone to do things for you? Is it that you feel like you shouldn't be able to receive if you give?

heart checks

- Are you a giver but have a hard time when it's your turn to receive?
- If so, why do you feel bad receiving?
- Do you have a hard time asking for what you need, such as help, gifts, or advice?

THE INITIATOR

T he number of misconceptions about humility go far beyond what we have mentioned here, but this is just a starter to get you thinking and considering other things we should be checking for within our hearts around the topic of humility and pride. Finding the less obvious aspects and considering them is essential as we strive to become all God has called us to be, while also laying aside everything that easily hinders us.

Remember to replace life's misconceptions with the truth. When we know better, we do better. As you continue examining your heart, add new misconceptions and truths that come to mind—ones we haven't covered in this book. Let's keep the list growing: Misconceptions vs Truth.

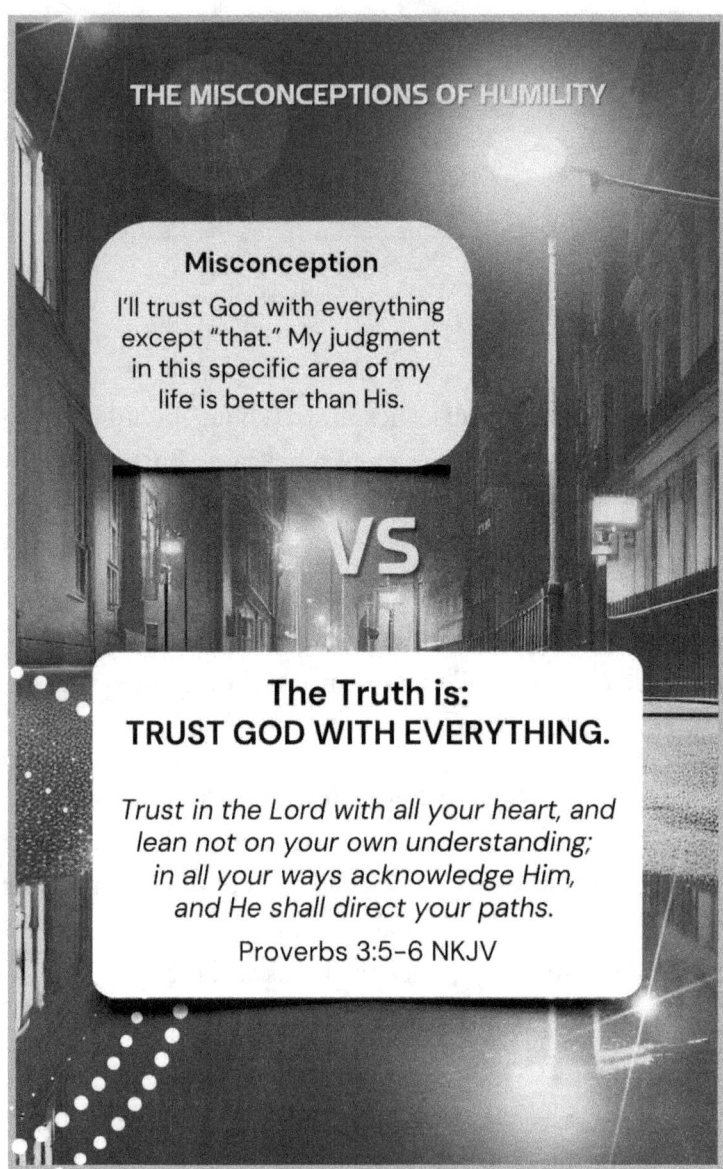

THE MISCONCEPTIONS OF HUMILITY

Misconception
I'll trust God with everything except "that." My judgment in this specific area of my life is better than His.

VS

The Truth is:
TRUST GOD WITH EVERYTHING.

Trust in the Lord with all your heart, and lean not on your own understanding; in all your ways acknowledge Him, and He shall direct your paths.

Proverbs 3:5-6 NKJV

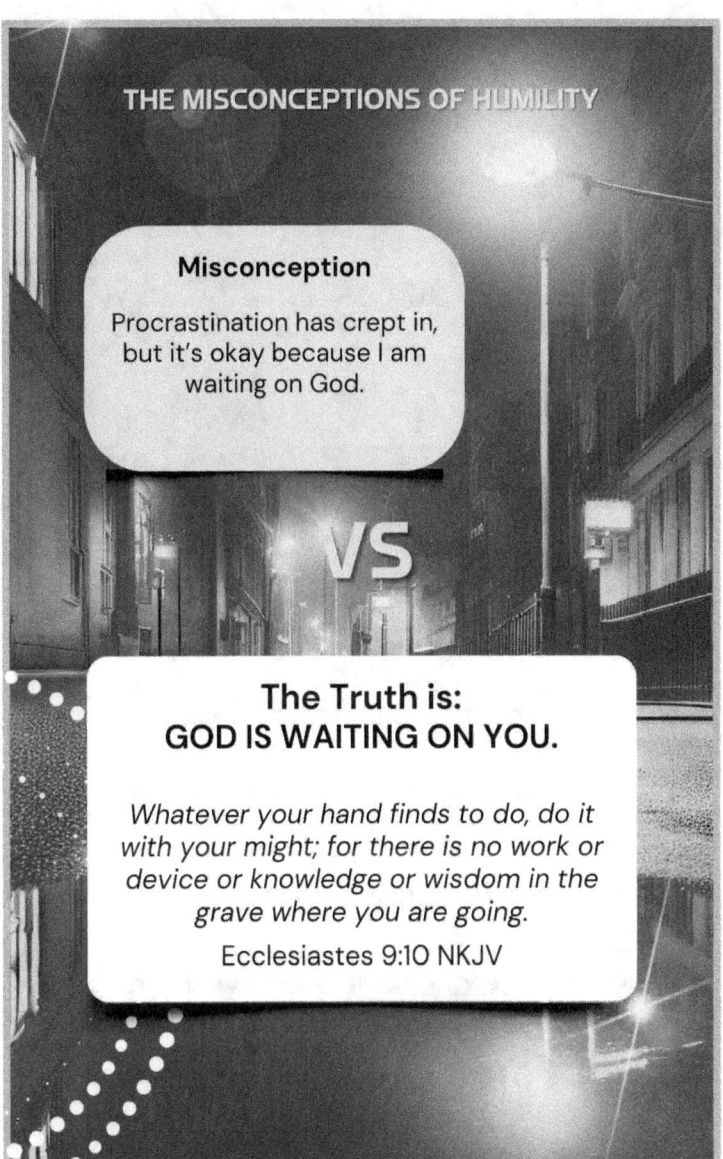

THE MISCONCEPTIONS OF HUMILITY

Misconception

Procrastination has crept in, but it's okay because I am waiting on God.

VS

The Truth is:
GOD IS WAITING ON YOU.

Whatever your hand finds to do, do it with your might; for there is no work or device or knowledge or wisdom in the grave where you are going.

Ecclesiastes 9:10 NKJV

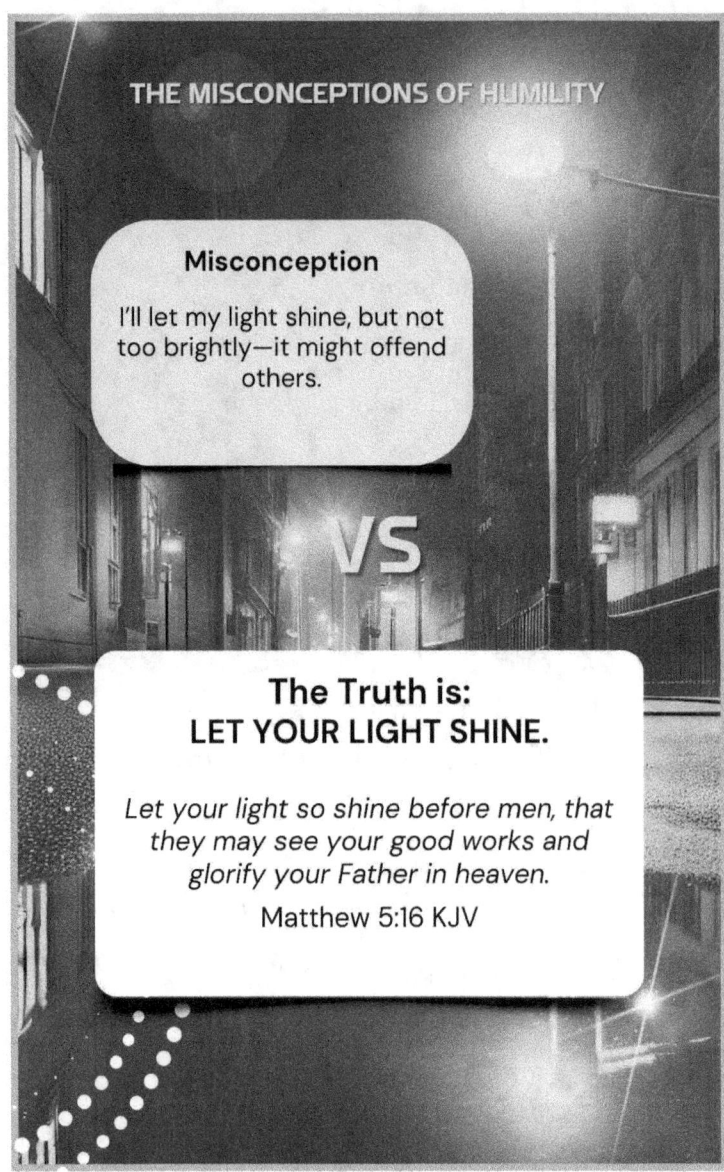

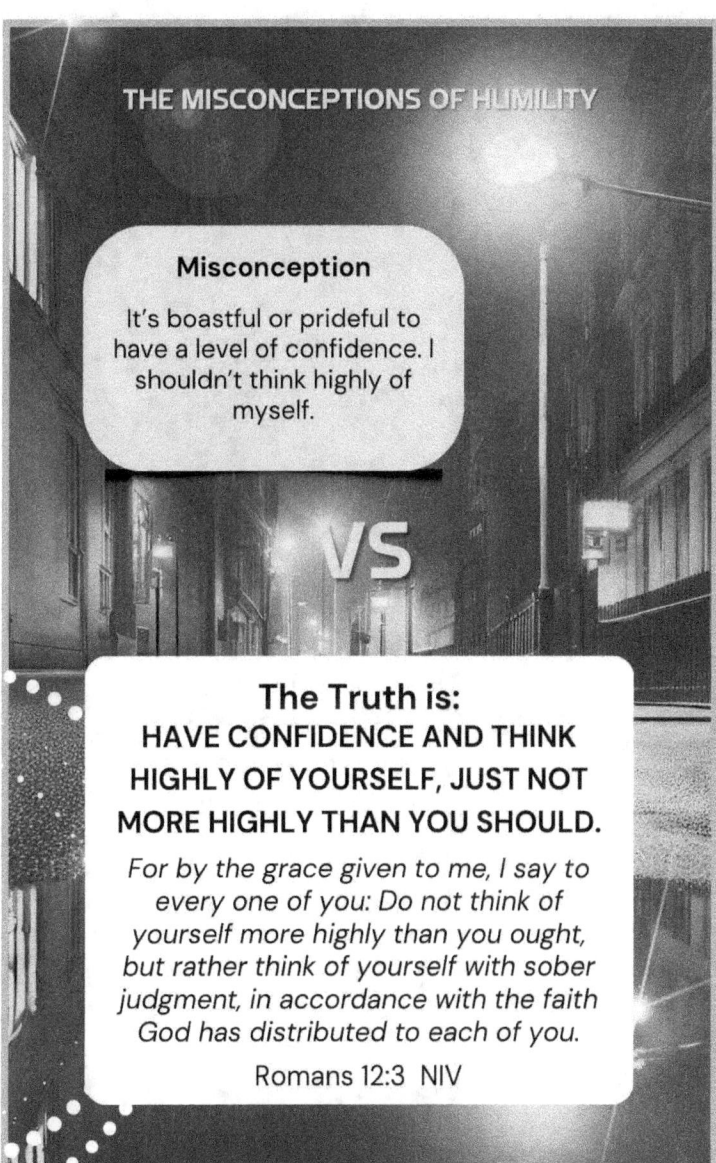

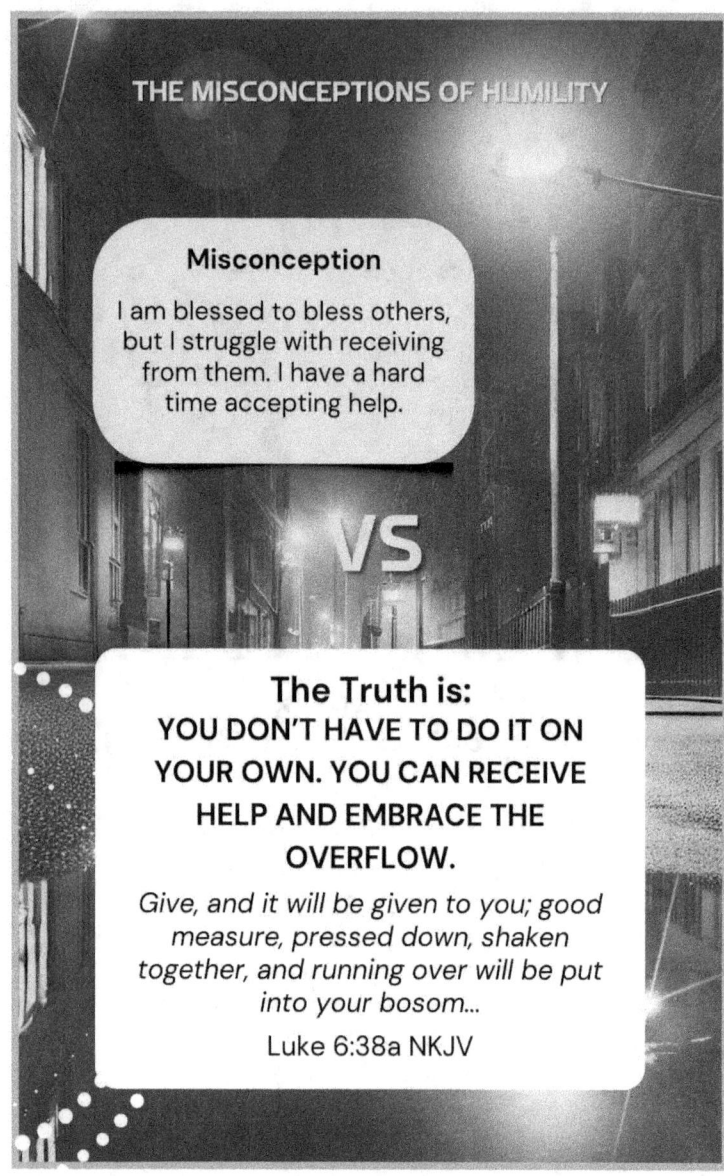

THE MISCONCEPTIONS OF HUMILITY

Misconception

I am blessed to bless others, but I struggle with receiving from them. I have a hard time accepting help.

VS

The Truth is:
YOU DON'T HAVE TO DO IT ON YOUR OWN. YOU CAN RECEIVE HELP AND EMBRACE THE OVERFLOW.

Give, and it will be given to you; good measure, pressed down, shaken together, and running over will be put into your bosom...

Luke 6:38a NKJV

Pride really is a tricky thing, and we want to constantly make sure we stay in a state of repentance as we live this thing called life. The very moment you need to check your pride is when you think you don't.

Trust God with your entire life, all the parts. He already knows from the beginning. All you have to do is be obedient. When trusting God, you don't always know the ins and outs, especially not beforehand. There is no point in trying to figure out your own life when you know the one who knows all of it. It is only through Christ that we can humble ourselves and truly stay at the foot of the throne. Staying before the Lord keeps us knowing it is all only by his grace and mercy.

PRAYER OF REPENTANCE

The following prayer is included for you to use as a guide to help you repent for engaging in any form of pride, regardless of how inconspicuous it may have been.

Heavenly Father, thank you. Thank you for your grace and mercy. Thank you for your love and kindness towards me. I enter into your gates with thanksgiving and your courts with praise. I come boldly before your throne of grace, asking you to forgive me. Forgive me for operating in pride and entertaining the misconceptions of humility in my life. You are the one true God, the Lord of lords, and I praise your name. Oh Lord, help me to keep you first in everything and in every area of my life. I trust you and ask as I read and study the Word of God, you continue to light my path and illuminate the hidden areas in my life that need to be dealt with. I love you, Lord, and thank you for loving me. Thank you for your patience with me and for always wanting the best for me.

It is in the name of Jesus Christ, I pray. Amen.

GUIDE ME BY MO JCKSN

The song "Guide Me" by the amazing Mo JCKSN perfectly captures my desire for Holy Spirit to guide me. Even before this song had verses, it would minister to me. (One of the perks to being around during the creative process, lol.) Although it was not written for me nor this book project, the lyrics put words to things I did not have the words to express, and the Lord knew beforehand both would be paired together. I am absolutely elated for you all to hear this song and for it to minister to you as well.

Mo describes her song *Guide Me* as a prayer, "A prayer for guidance from the God of Abraham, Isaac, and Jacob, Jehovah. It's a song that describes the feeling many people experience at different points in life—a feeling of not knowing the right decision to make or what to do in certain situations. It's a simple prayer asking God to lead and guide you, as the scripture supports, if you ask God for guidance or clarity, He'll answer and lead you. He's faithful."

If you have not received your very own copy of the song "Guide Me," which was included with your purchase of this book, go to **www.misconceptionsofhumility.com** or scan the QR code below to complete the form.

To access your copy of the single "Guide Me" by Mo JCKSN, scan the QR code. or visit www.MisconceptionsofHumility.com to complete the form and follow the instructions.

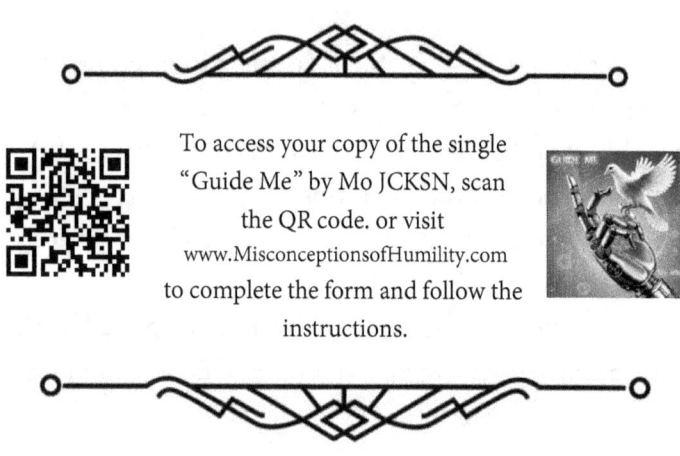

I am so grateful to God for Mo JCKSN and the gift she is to my life. Thank you, Mo, for partnering with me and allowing your song "Guide Me" to accompany this book, *The Misconceptions of Humility*. We both know what it took to get here, haha, and I am forever grateful for you. May God bless and may you reap a great harvest from the seeds you have sown and for the continued blessing you are to not only me but the masses through your heart for people, your love for God, and your many gifts and talents.

Be sure to show her some love and check out her upcoming projects at **www.mojcksn.com**.

ABOUT THE AUTHOR

Kartriece Ward is a passionate servant leader with over a decade of experience helping visionaries bring their ideas and dreams to life. By the grace of God, her heart for service shines through in every area of her life, whether through her creative pursuits, traveling, or spending cherished moments with her family.

Now a first-time author with The Misconceptions of Humility, Kartriece shares a profound message rooted in her Christian faith, encouraging readers to embrace true humility by depending on God's grace rather than succumbing to false modesty.

Kartriece is also the host of the podcast Serve Well 24/7, where she inspires listeners to lead lives centered on serving others with excellence. As a dynamic speaker, she is passionate about sharing insights on service, faith, and purpose at events and engagements nationwide.

Through her work, Kartriece aims to empower others to live lives of Christ-like humility, service, and impact.

Stay connected via social media and sign up for her email list at www.kartrieceward.com

For U.S. press inquiries regarding
The Misconceptions of Humility,
or to book Kartriece Ward for speaking engagements
please email hello@kartrieceward.com.

www.ingramcontent.com/pod-product-compliance
Lightning Source LLC
Chambersburg PA
CBHW052206070526
44585CB00017B/2097